G000109537

Branches of my Tree

Exploring the essence of life

instagram.com/branchesofmytree

First edition

This edition published in 2021

 First published by
HULLO CREATIVE LTD.
www.hullocreative.com

Copyright © Deem Mirza 2021

All rights reserved. No portion of this book may be reproduced,
stored in a retrieval system, or transmitted in any form or by any means,
(mechanical, electronic, photocopying, recording, or otherwise),
without written permission from the copyright owner and publisher.
Tree illustrations by Polly Wyer

Photographs sourced from Shutterstock and Unsplash

ISBN 978-0-9935366-6-3

Branches
of my Tree

Exploring the essence of life

DEEM MIRZA

To my dearest husband.

Thank you for walking alongside me,
as I made my dreams a reality.

Contents

Foreword

Foreword

Branches of my Tree is the musings of a woman – mother, wife, daughter, sister. Moments in time, feelings captured in words.

The author is my mother. The title of the book talks of her network of connections, and the aspects of her life that are rooted in her individualism, serving as a support to the branches that spread and grow as she does. These vignettes of life are particularly special because they're derived from her personal experiences throughout her childhood and into her adult life, from leaving her hometown to navigating the trials of marriage and motherhood in an unfamiliar culture.

Her experiences are both unique and incredibly relatable in their wider context; they bring a well-rounded perspective to her work, welcoming a wide audience. Combined with her talents as a writer, readers can feel like each piece was personally written for them.

Having shared part of this journey with her, at times being an observant onlooker to her work, I can say that every piece was written with purpose: products of her insights as they arrived, not contrived for the sake of content.

Opening up these moments to the eyes of the world invites people to peer into the instances of personal growth and self-discovery, taking from it what they wish.

Branches of my Tree encapsulates the delicate and nuanced aspects of our emotional lives that we might not otherwise address; the difficulties and rewards of family and relationships are celebrated; readers can take comfort in her words and find their own sense of familiarity.

Shorter than prose but more robust than poetry, each passage gives you something to linger over, providing some food for thought. But this you can only appreciate by reading the book.

Growing Up

Shattered glass

Once, as a little girl, I accidentally broke a beautiful vase.
It was completely shattered. My uncle rushed in and
started yelling at me for being clumsy and naughty, just
as my grandma came in to see if I was ok and whether
I had hurt my hand.

There are always two kinds of people in this world:
the ones who care about the glass and the ones who
care about your hand.

Piggy-back ride

A tiny line appeared on his brow every time he said,
"No worry, baby; no worry." I didn't worry because my dad
took all the worry away. I was free to conquer the world
and I did. I knew he would pick me up any time I fell.

He taught me to fly kites, train dogs, drive a car and many
more of life's lessons. He was firm on occasions and soft
on others, but always called a spade a spade.

He taught me everything I know and continues to impart
his wise worldly advice. With him, I'm still the little girl
asking for another piggy-back ride.

The Hand of God

As a little girl, whilst being driven along the coastline,
I would look up at the sky and get blinded by the sunlight.

Sometimes I would see the rays shine through the clouds.
I would imagine myself floating through the rays and
reaching for the Hand of God. If I were lucky enough
to hold it, my body would feel a charged sensation and
a renewed confidence. I knew I could hold anything
as long as God was holding my hand.

Life lessons my mama taught me

My mother taught me to be kind.
My mother taught me to be humble.
My mother taught me to be persevering.
My mother taught me to be graceful and dignified.
My mother taught me to love life and always be positive.

My mother taught me all this leading by example.

Today my mum is teaching me how to be brave and fight;
and I know this too will be a successful lesson of our lives.

Dearest Dad

When I was little, I saw you as physically strong, a superhero who loved dogs, cars, photography and sports.

As I grew up I realised those qualities had a deeper meaning. You are strong both physically but also in principle.

Your love of dogs showed me how to care for all things living. Your love of cars showed me how to enjoy the finer things in life. Your love of photography taught me how to capture and appreciate beauty. Your love of sports taught me to be fair and a team player.

You are and always will be my superhero.

Anytime

"You've ruined my life! I'm leaving!" I shouted as I stormed out the door. Oh, it felt so good to be free at last! I was walking on the clouds and singing in the rain.

Just as I stopped to smell the roses, I missed her. Roses are her favourite flowers. I could see the concern behind her raised brows and hear the joy behind her cackle.

"I want to come home mum," I texted.

She responded instantly: "Anytime."

Happily Ever After?

I won't let you fall

As I walked down the aisle toward him, my 20-something footsteps faltered a bit. He walked towards me and gently took my hand in his. "I won't let you fall," he whispered in my ear. We've walked alongside each other for decades now; sometimes I hold his hand and sometimes he holds mine. Anytime our steps falter I whisper to him,
"I won't let you fall."

My lost world

I walked into his life thinking, "I want to be his whole world." Over time his family became my family. His friends became my friends. His likes and dislikes became my likes and dislikes. His choices became my choices.

As I look back, I realise that in the hope of becoming his whole world, I lost mine.

Why should I buy the eggs?

As I unloaded the groceries from my car, I made a mental list of things I need to do: pick up the laundry, take the dog to the vet, take our son to the orthodontist appointment and then sort dinner. The day was full.

I took the groceries to the kitchen – the rain had made them damp so I wanted to quickly unpack.

My husband walked in and glanced around. "Oh, you forgot the eggs," he remarked.

I stopped and inhaled deeply.

"I did forget them," I replied coolly. "Perhaps next time you can fit grocery shopping into your schedule."

Farewell to hearts

Relationships are complicated at the best of times. Our most important relationship is with ourselves – we cannot be fair to anyone if we are not true to our core.

We adapt and mould us to circumstances, people and situations but if we don't act from our inner self we will always end up unhappy.

I want to be true to myself and set you free.

I want to cherish good times as a beautiful reminder of my youth.

I want the memory of our relationship to shine forever.

It's just a farewell of hearts – I can't have mine broken again.

Happily ever after

Lucky are those for whom happily ever after becomes
a reality; some of us are just content with the rhythm of
everyday life. Our happily ever after is in our own hands –
we can either live it or blame someone for not having it.

Putting our hopes and dreams on our partners is not part
of the deal, yet somehow, during the courtship, we lead
ourselves to believe that it is.

We are the makers of our own destiny – so step up
and make our own happily ever after. Who said you
need a partner to do it?

Being a Mum

Being a Mum

I have the honour and pleasure of being a mum to four horribly gorgeous, yet fantastically different young adults. Needless to say, life with them has been one hell of a roller coaster. From their first words to their first swear words, from their toy cars to their real cars, we have gone through many ups and downs.

Being a mum is not easy; most days I haven't a clue what I'm doing. The day starts, life begins and before I can catch a breath, it starts all over again.

I gave up being Mum of the Year ages ago. Most days I am just content with being Mum of the Hour.

Don't tell me how to raise my child!

You didn't see me up all night. You didn't see her take
her first steps. You didn't witness the parking lot tantrum.

You didn't watch her prep school graduation.

You didn't see the excitement of her first crush.
You didn't see the sadness of her first heartbreak.
You didn't hear "I hate you; you ruined my life."
You didn't get the best-mum-in-the-world hug.

So don't tell me how to raise my child; not until
you've had your own.

Lemons

"Don't eat lemons, they irritate your tummy," I said,
as my daughter reached out to grab a slice. She knows
not to eat them now. Every time she makes a choice,
she turns around for my approval.

I've taught you everything I know; I taught you
everything I learnt. You have to make your own
choices now. You don't need my approval – I trust
your choices. I know you won't choose lemons.

My little angel

She sat in the corner with her head bowed. I went and sat next to her as she turned her tear-streaked face towards me.

"We broke up," she whispered.

I wanted to kiss her broken heart better. I held her hand as she leant her head on my shoulder and let the tears fall silently.

You will get through this, my little angel, but for now just let the pain flow.

I respectfully disagree

Yesterday my 12-year-old was very angry with his friend.
His friend did not share the same opinion as him.

I took this opportunity to explain the bigger picture
to my son. We are all entitled to our views and opinions
and should be able to communicate them effectively.
The question is not about right or wrong, rather it's about
respecting human sentiments. Arguments seldom lead to
solutions. Discussions, however, are a healthier alternative.

Whenever we choose to disagree with an opinion,
we should remember to do it respectfully.

I see you

I see your quiet smile; I see your teary eye. I see you
sitting silently while the house is rushing by. I see you
when you think no one is looking; I see you when you
whisper your wishes. I see you every day, whether you
are busy with life or just lost in your thoughts.

Your voice may be lost in this noisy world, but my child,
I see in you the fire to be seen.

Why do you care? It's my life!

I have been asked this question many times as my children have grown up. I've pondered over it and thought, why do I care? Do I care because I'm their mother? Do I care just because I gave birth to them? Do I care because that's all I've done since they came into my life?

Yes, I care because that's all I've known. I care because when the tiny bundle was placed in my arms, I made a promise to always love and protect it. The cord may have been severed but the bond of care wasn't. So my child, why do I care? Because I love you.

Stop!

STOP telling me what to do!
STOP telling me what to wear!
STOP telling me who to see!
STOP telling me when to come home!
STOP telling me how to live my life!
STOP! Just STOP!
I'm an adult now and I will do as I please!

I know you are, my child. I'm just waiting
for you to say it, not shout it.

The last time

I remember my child's first steps; I don't remember
the last time I carried her in my lap. I remember
the first time a tiny hand clutched my finger; I don't
remember the last time it let go. I remember her first
words; I don't remember the last time I read to her.

If I had known the last time was the last time,
I would have held on longer.

Man, Woman,
Boy, Girl

Let the little boy cry

Grown men were little boys once. While growing up they learnt not to cry because "boys don't cry".

The way to heal is going through the pain. We teach our boys to "be strong" and "toughen up" but we discourage tears.

Let them cry! They become "stronger" and "tougher" by feeling their pain. Tears heal – so let them flow; let the little boy cry.

For as beautiful as a glowing ember looks, it burns everything that touches it.

What's inside the handbag?

The most important accessory for many women is the handbag. It's important to get it just right to complete the look. The colour, the style, the shape, the size – everything is considered before making that ultimate choice.

But what intrigues me is the contents that go inside the handbag. A quick glance as someone hastily opens their handbag gives an insight into the kind of person they are. Organised? Always prepared? Sloppy? Smoker? Drinker? The list is endless.

Whatever we choose to show the world through our fabulous label and style, we must remember that it is what's inside the handbag that reveals who we truly are.

The length of a skirt

Women are not commodities to be passed on from
fathers to husbands. They are individuals in their own
right. They don't belong to anybody, their purpose is
not just procreation and nurturing future generations.
They have hopes and dreams and ambitions too.
They too have the right to freedom.

It is imperative to teach our men not to value
women by the length of their skirts.

You're a boy - it's not your fault

You were raised to believe you are superior – it's not your fault.
You grew up thinking you were better – it's not your fault.
You saw your mother and sisters do your chores – it's not your fault.
You were told you are a boy and that's enough – it's not your fault.

Today you are a man and a father.
What will you teach your son?
Because that will all be your fault.

In the line of fire

I fought for my mother; I fought for my sisters.
I fought for my friends; I fought for their friends.
I fought for my daughters; I fought for the injustices
done to all women on the planet.

One day they said to me, "We didn't ask you to fight for us."
It was then that I realised I was only ever fighting for some
part of me.

It's too late for me to put my weapons down;
I am the warrior, always in the line of fire.

If you had just...

If you had just looked away, you could
have avoided his lewd gaze.
If you had just covered properly,
he would not have been tempted
to behave inappropriately.
If you had just played your cards right,
the job would have been yours.
If you had just raised them right,
your daughters would not
speak their mind.
If you had just toed the line.

If you had just smiled and never
questioned this entitled
authority of mine.

The girl in the box

At birth I was placed in the 'girl' box. It was pretty
and pink and lined with silk. It had ruffles and frills
and filled with all girly things.

At adolescence, the box changed a bit. They added dolls
and kitchen sets, bangles and anklets. I moved them aside
to make room for my karate belts and medals. I filled my
box with rocks and slingshots, with spitballs and whistles.
The box was old and had to break its traditional mould.

In my adulthood, the box had marriage and motherhood.
I added a career and self-care. I added me before you and,
to the horror of the generation above, I broke that box too.

Now the universe placed an angel in my arms.
I looked at her smiling face and said
"Granny has broken all of your boxes for you."

Friendship

Learning to remain silent

Conversation is the best tool for communication. Generations of people communicate through it. But staying silent is an acquired skill. The ones that master it are usually the best conversationalists.

Just as a picture speaks a thousand words, silence communicates a thousand emotions.

Last night I let a tear slip

Last night I let a tear slip and the world was quick to judge.
My storms knew no boundaries as they lashed inside me.
I tried to hold it in, but amidst the laughter a tear escaped.
Everyone around was eager to spread the word:
My life wasn't perfect!

Two angels guided me through the darkness and took me
to a side. I wept my heart out. I leant my head against
her shoulder while the other stroked my hair.

Last night I let a tear slip and found true friendship.

Let's leave them alone

More often than not, when a loved one is behaving out of character or in a way we deem not right, our general conclusion is to leave them alone. They'll get over it if we give them time. We tend to convince ourselves that time and space is what a person needs to gain perspective.

In reality, what they probably need most at that point is us. Our presence can help a loved one through turmoil; we don't necessarily need to fix the problem, just hear it. Next time, before giving someone space, make some in your heart.

Over a cup of coffee

I saw two women sitting at a cafe; I think they were friends.
They were engrossed in deep conversation with the
occasional burst of laughter, leaning towards each other
and sometimes whispering secrets.

As the steam from their coffee cups rose and brightened
their already lit faces, I thought to myself: sometimes all
we need in life is that special person to have coffee with.

The ginger in my life

I met a leprechaun and his name was ginger!
His cheeky grin and sweet disposition provided
a magical comfort. He brightened my day even after
the darkest of nights. His encouraging words and
persistent demeanour help me achieve my personal
best. Our mutual love for all things sweet makes me
feel he is the exceptional spice in my simple life.

Relationships that strengthen us

My cousin visited me after a long, long time. As we embraced each other, our eyes moistened at the familiarity of the touch. We had grown up in the same house. To me he was my older brother, my friend, my confidant. Even though we met after two decades, the connection was instant.

We spent a few hours together and filled each other in on our lives. I valued this relationship that strengthened me. As we said our goodbyes, I felt fuller; just like a baby who has had a satisfying feed.

Sis, I miss you

You left your shirt behind. It fits me fine – your scent
lingers on it and your warmth too. I put it on and
felt you hug me tight.

You left your tub of lip gloss too, it has the
indentations of your fingertips. It reminded me
of your gentle touch and your kisses on my brow.

I messaged you to let you know, but what I wanted
to say was: Oh sis, I miss you so.

Farewell, my friend

I have found goodbyes difficult. This one in particular is exceptionally hard. I feel the finality of it stronger than the ones before. The comfort of knowing you're down the road will be no more. The last minute breakfast plans and the freezing morning walks are memories I will cherish the most. Our random phone calls and spontaneous visits for a quick chat will be missed so much.

I will miss you.

Farewell my friend, I wish you every happiness.

Moments
in Time

Rays of hope

As the sky at dawn turns a warm pink, my heart feels
a warmer glow. A new day! A new chance at life. A day
to right the wrong. A day to say hello, again. A day to
warm my palms with a hot mug of tea.

As I watch the sun rise, the rays of hope rise in me too.

Sunday morning runners

I decided to go for a run early this Sunday morning,
mainly because I wanted to run out of the house.
On my way, I passed other early morning runners
and couldn't help but wonder what had brought them
out. Were they running off a hangover? Were they
running away from something, or towards it?
Were they merely health nuts who didn't even rest
on Sundays? Or were they looking for an excuse
to run away from someone?

Lost in my trail of thoughts, I found myself back
at my front door. My run was over. Fumbling for my
door keys, I smiled: we all have our reasons to run,
but how long until they catch us up?

Today I climbed a tree

Today I climbed a tree. As I let the strong branches cradle me, my burdens seemed to lighten a little. The sun warmed my back and my thoughts floated to my childhood. I heard my sister's laughter and a dog barking playfully. I felt a lightness in my body that warmed me to my core.

"Let's go mum!" said my son, and woke me from my stupor. For just a moment, I had the feeling of bliss; the same one we get when we've just woken up and the world is perfect. I will hold on to this and every now again climb a tree with my loved ones.

Sometimes storms are
sent to save us

The recent storms and weather conditions
left us all housebound.

After the initial bickering and disappointments
of having missed certain events, the family
settled around the fireplace. We decided
to get out a good old board game, make some
hot chocolate and toast the marshmallows.
We reconnected and bonded with each other
over silly stories and simple jokes.

As I looked around the room at their glowing
faces, a thought arose in my mind: sometimes
storms are sent to save us, not destroy us.

Hope in the time of a pandemic

I woke up this morning to the sounds of ambulance sirens and wondered which family was struck this time. My heart said a silent prayer for them, as I thought of my own family spread across the globe. I pray for their safety, worry about their health and wonder: when will I hug them again?

Just then, my son jumps on my bed informing me about our dog's latest trick. I wipe my silent tears and smile at the blessings around me. As I hug my son close to me, I remind myself never to lose hope no matter how hard times get.

Of pearls and pendants but mostly independence

My fingers brushed against a delicate string of pearls as
I was rummaging through my jewellery bowl searching for
my favourite pendant. I took them out and placed them
around my neck; admired their colour against my skin.
I remember being told, "Pearls are for special occasions!"

Well, today is a special occasion: I am celebrating me.
My choices, my eccentricities, my flaws, my manners,
my kindness, my acceptance, my beauty, my age, my
colour, my heritage.

Today I am celebrating me and there couldn't be
a better occasion for pearls.

The huddle

Friday evening, as the sun settles for the day, a group of boys huddle before the match. The team spirit and unity brightens the evening even more. This camaraderie lasts a lifetime! The friendships formed on the fields are everlasting bonds.

How important is it for us to tell our children to 'play well' as it's only then where they learn to play fair and strong.

The huddle is the beginning of a great life.

The windows from my room

I look out my window and across the road
I see four more.

One has a young couple ever so in love.
The second has a young lady, her little dog and
friends visiting from time to time.
The third has a family with two children, rising
early each morning and leaving for school.
The fourth has an elderly couple playing
their game of cards.

My windows used to look like each of those,
now all I have is a deck of cards.

Gratitude

As I cleared the dishes today and then folded the laundry
for my family, I felt genuine gratitude for my father.
I smiled silently as his words echoed in my mind:
learn to adapt to all situations, happily.

Life recently threw a curved ball at me and instead of
dodging it, I played it! While my family struggled, I
remembered my father's advice and adapted to the new
situation. From having freshly laundered clothes delivered
to my door step to ironing my own shirts, I was able to
make the smooth transition.

Sometimes when we despise our parents for their life
lessons, we need to take a deep breath and make a mental
note. For one day, we will be grateful for them.

Life's Truths

When want to's become have to's

Our deepest desires and needs drive us to strive
for achievement. The world is magical and our
journey is exciting.

Once we have achieved our wants, our hearts pause
a minute. Our breath slows down and the rush of
adrenaline subsides. Over time our wants become
hindrances to our life. They are the cumbersome
have to's that make our existence drag.

Somewhere between our want to's and have to's,
we lose the zeal for living.

Success

Success is getting an award for our achievements.
Success is teaching our child to say their first words.
Success is persevering against all odds.
Success is never facing failure.
Success is continuing in spite of failure.

For some of us, success is simply getting out of bed
each day, not knowing if anything is possible.

Walking around with mirrors

There is no right or wrong, just different perceptions of the same issue. A mirror reverses our reflection and shows our right as left. In life, if we were able to look at our right as someone else's left, many issues would be resolved.

Unfortunately, not many can look past the shadow of ego to see the other side. The bigger our ego, the further it pushes us from relationships.

Life could be a whole lot simpler if we walked around with mirrors.

The familiarity of it all

Some days when life overwhelms me with itself, I find solace in things that are familiar. The familiarity of his scent on the pillow; the familiarity of his snores at night. The familiarity of footsteps; the familiarity of arguments. The familiarity of appliances whirring around; the familiarity as my home settles for the evening.

Life is not without challenges but, in the end, as long as I have my familiarity around me I will prosper.

Do we break traditions or do traditions break us?

I often ask myself why I do certain things the way I do them. More often than not it's because that's how Mum or Grandma did them. Sometimes it works and sometimes it doesn't – they did it at a time when tradition was convenient to their lives. I was asked to follow it, but never had the reasons explained to me.

I am now making my own traditions, traditions that I would like my children to take forward – but only as long as they are not a burden for them.

We need to break traditions before they break us.

My elements of anger

When my anger is red – it is hot and bright, like
the flames that rage and surely burn with spite.
When my anger is brown – I am stuck in the ground;
every grudge I hold is visible in my frown.
When my anger is green – my life is unfair and
I find great happiness in despair.
When my anger is blue – I am sad to my soul,
I lament and cry enough to fill an Olympic sized pool.
When my anger is black – it is ready to tear, it sounds
like thunder, often leaving me without air.

Whatever colour or element my anger takes, I am
pained to see the destruction caused in its wake.

Nothing changes except our attitude

Recent events in my life have led me to a conclusion:
People don't want to be saved.
People don't want to be helped.
People don't want our advice.
They just want to be heard!

So I decided to listen.

Life moves at its own pace and on its own clock.
We have to learn to adjust to it; it won't adjust to us.

In the end nothing will help us more than adapting
to the situation we are faced with. So change nothing
but your attitude.

Let the scales tip

My life is increasingly becoming a balancing act.
I try to balance all aspects in my daily routine.
From balance meals to balance diaries, I cover
the entire spectrum.

However, some days I find balancing my cheque
book easier than balancing my life – and math
is not my strong point!

But then the scales tip.

The tight rope I walk on each day does cause my
feet to hurt and they do slip into pitfalls.
What is the right balance? How do I strike it?
How much is too much?

I feel, sometimes it is better to let the scales tip,
because only then can we regain our balance.

When the lights dim

This pandemic has taught me a new way of living.
Things I had learned had to be unlearned and relearned.
I had thought that as we age life would get into a
comfortable rhythm but I had to change my rhythm.

When I was younger, I remember visiting the cinema for
the first time with my parents. I remember the excitement
and the thrill of watching the feature film. Arms laden with
popcorn and soda, we took our seats and stared at the screen,
waiting for the film to begin – then the lights went dim.

Confused at what was happening, I looked towards my Dad.
He told me we were being prepared for the start of the film.
The hall went quiet, the screen enlarged and the movie started.

The pandemic did not give me a warning; I wish it had
dimmed the lights so I could have prepared to start my film.

I choose to look at...

As the curtain draws on another year, I look on in amazement at all the opportunities the last 12 months have provided me.

We can look back at our life and mourn our losses but I choose to look at the paths that opened up as a result.

I choose to look at my personal growth. I choose to look at the everlasting bonds of friendship I formed. I choose to look at my garden's seasonal bloom. I choose to look at the circumstances which reduced negative influences on my life.

I choose to look at my resolve at forever choosing the bright side of life.

The Passage
of Time

Ages, phases, stages

Ages, phases, stages – from birth we are going through them. They shape us, they break us and then remake us.

It is a continuous process of growth. Some people evolve, some get stuck and some progressively regress.

It is intriguing to acknowledge our own process of evolution: certain beliefs we had in our early age definitely changed at a later stage. The phases we went through gave birth to new aspects of our personality.

My own experiences taught me that rigidity is futile and flexibility is the way of life. We are yet again in a new stage of life and I am curious to see which way we will grow this time.

The front door

The front door of my home was robust and strong
10 years ago. The main reason for this (apart from it being
new) was that my children could not reach the handle.
Now, the hinges and lock can barely hold it together.
Countless times it has been slammed shut. I have bid them
farewell and stayed up until all hours of the night as they
fumbled with keys or texted each other to silently let them in.

My front door has weathered many storms, endured
many kicks and held its tongue about many a secret.
It has seen my children and their friends pass through it,
laughing; overheard fights and apologies knowing they
would happen again. My front door has done this patiently,
sometimes creaking, or becoming stuck and refusing
to let anyone in or out.

It is no longer as shiny and polished as when we first
bought it. The tales of time are visible in its wood and
the edges are frayed. But it has always stood straight and
firm in its place and my children know once they walk
in through the front door, they are safe and home.

The dresser that belonged to my grandmother

As I was clearing the attic of old junk I came across a
dresser which belonged to my grandmother. My daughter
and I dusted it and cleaned the stained mirror. As we stared
at our reflection, I caught a glimpse of my grandma.
Her majestic stance and dignified manner made me smile
with pride. Her determination and courage always amazed
me as a little girl.

I looked at my daughter's reflection and wondered if
she too could feel the lineage of strong women standing
right behind her.

Roller coaster of time

The struggles of life keep coming and going – some leave us depleted of emotions while some help us discover our unknown strengths.

The fascinating aspect in this roller coaster of situations is that life keeps moving on. Days pass into months and years. What may have seemed as an impossible time to get by becomes a nebulous memory of sorts.

The grace and dignity with which we carry ourselves through a crisis forms our character, and that is something which only gets stronger with time.

I want you around

We walked together, hand in hand, mine smaller in hers.
My steps were quick and eager, stumbling every now and
then. Her grip was gentle yet secure. We went to the store
to buy some clothes. She showed me many and I fussed and
frowned. I want what I want, you don't have to be around!

We walked together hand in hand, mine firmer than hers.
My steps were paced and measured, firm as I walked beside
her. I held her hand while guiding her through the store.
She tugged me ever so slightly, "I would like to sit a bit,
my knees aren't keeping up," she said with a smile. I sat
next to her and held her tightly. I'm not going anywhere,
if you promise to always be around.

When I was so busy looking ahead...

When I was so busy looking ahead, I couldn't see what was right in front of me. Special moments of life passed me by as I was striving for a supposedly secure future.

I don't know when my children became old enough to move out; the emptiness of their rooms reminded me of their endless chatter. I realised the future was here. My greying temples and worry lines were a harsh reminder of the time gone by.

I was so busy looking ahead, I forgot to live in the present.

The agony of ageing

My parents are ageing. I am ageing. My children are ageing. Being part of a sandwich generation is not as easy as I had envisaged. Just like I was not given a guide to raise children, I do not have a guide to cope with ageing parents. Things that once came easily to them are now their daily challenges, words which were once funny now sound insensitive, sounds which were once pleasant are now irritating.

No one explains the complexity of getting older. We try our best to do our best. Be kind to yourself; be gentle with yourself. Don't let the critical voices in our head lead us, for we too are going through the agony of ageing.

My hands hadn't changed, they had just aged

The flow of the water hadn't changed. The slippery suds of the soap hadn't changed. The newborn in my hands was as wriggly as her mum had been, some 20-odd years ago.

My hands hadn't changed, but their grip was sturdier, their movements more confident. They expertly moved around my granddaughter, washing and soaping her.

My hands hadn't changed, they had just aged.

Zooming through life

My world has changed.

My day started with a Zoom call to my family.
Followed by a Zoom yoga class. I checked on my
children in their Zoom lessons. Sometimes I attend
Zoom tutorials and on occasion have also attended
Zoom parties and weddings.

But today I attended a Zoom funeral. The pain was
unbearable, the helplessness unimaginable, the tears
uncontrollable.

Today I attended a Zoom funeral and I haven't
been able to leave the meeting.

Death is the only reality of life

Life is too short to love and too long to hate.

So make that phone call, send that text. Tell your loved ones how much you love them. We are lucky to sleep in our warm beds at night so make the most of it; you never know the next night could be in your grave.

Death is the only reality of life. Embrace what is there and let go of what is not.

*"When you practice gratefulness,
there is a sense of respect towards others"*

– Dalai Lama

Acknowledgements

I am truly humbled and grateful to all those who have helped in turning my dream into a reality. The Branches of my Tree have been watered by many wonderful people, the ones I mention below and the ones captured in my writing.

Dave Perkins and Hayley Kyte, thank you for your perseverance and patience while dealing with my delayed deadlines. You and your team at Hullo Creative nurtured the sapling so well that the tree now stands tall and strong. For all your efforts I thank you.

Polly Wyer, your wonderful illustrations are a visual delight and exactly how I had imagined my tree to be. Thank you for the work on the design of the book.

The difficult job of trimming and pruning was so skilfully managed by Rin Hamburgh and her talented team – thank you for editing the book so well. And finally a huge thank you to Andrea Sexton at Admire PR for helping me reach new hearts and minds across various continents.

Finally, dear Reader, thank you for sharing my thoughts. I hope I have successfully translated my essence of life.

About the author

Deem Mirza is the pen name of Fabiha Haq, a Pakistani British writer, special education teacher, social and welfare worker, yogi and human rights supporter.

Born in 1975, she has spent her life interacting with diverse cultures, religions and social strata, and is a fervent believer in equality, resilience, physical and mental wellbeing, and forgiveness. She values human relationships, cultural and religious nuances, and being open to challenging and changing rigid, stereotypical concepts of our existence.

Branches of my Tree reflects Fabiha's unique style of writing, which connects the reader with the delicate and deeper meaning of life, relationships, wellbeing and spiritual connectivity.

You can find more of her writings on Instagram at @branchesofmytree

Lightning Source UK Ltd.
Milton Keynes UK
UKHW050252250921
391104UK00005B/82/J